ANIMALS

Bats

by Kevin Holmes

Content Consultant:
Robert Benson, Public Information Officer
Bat Conservation International

Bridgestone Books
an imprint of Capstone Press

Bridgestone Books are published by Capstone Press,
151 Good Counsel Drive, P.O. Box 669, Mankato, Minnesota 56002.
www.capstonepress.com

Library of Congress Cataloging-in-Publication Data
Holmes, Kevin J.
    Bats/by Kevin J. Holmes.
    p. cm.--(Animals)
    Includes bibliographical references (p. 23) and index.
    Summary: An introduction to bats, covering their physical characteristics, habits, prey, and
relationship to humans.
    ISBN-13: 978-1-56065-602-9 (hardcover)   ISBN-10: 1-56065-602-6 (hardcover)
    ISBN-13: 978-0-7368-8069-5 (softcover pbk.)   ISBN-10: 0-7368-8069-0 (softcover pbk.)
    1. Bats--Juvenile literature. [1. Bats.] I. Title. II. Series: Animals (Mankato, Minn.)
QL737.C5H57 1998
599.4--dc21

                                                                        97-12204
                                                                            CIP
                                                                            AC

Photo credits
Bat Conservation International, 6; Bat Conservation International/Merlin Tuttle, 10, 12, 14, 16, 18
James Rowan, 20
Kirsty Zahnke, 8
Visuals Unlimited/John D. Cunningham, cover

2 3 4 5 6 04 03 02 01 00

Table of Contents

Photo Diagram 4
Fast Facts 5

Bats 7
Appearance 9
Where Bats Live 11
Sight and Sound 13
Food 15
Enemies 17
Young Bats 19
Bats and People 21

Hands On: Echolocation 22
Words to Know 23
Read More 23
Useful Addresses 24
Internet Sites 24
Index 24

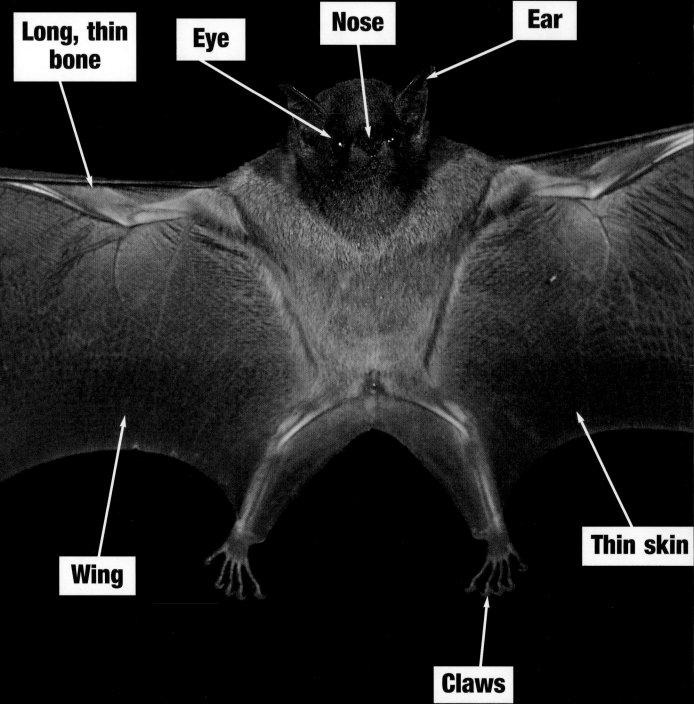

Long, thin bone

Eye

Nose

Ear

Wing

Thin skin

Claws

Fast Facts

Kinds: There are more than 900 different kinds of bats all around the world. Each kind of bat has its own features.

Range: Bats live in most countries of the world. They do not live in places that become very hot or cold.

Habitat: Bats live in attics, caves, and inside hollow tree trunks. Some bats live in tree branches.

Food: Bats eat many different things. Some eat fruit juices or flower juices. Others eat fruit. Some eat bugs, fish, lizards, and frogs. Some bats drink other animals' blood.

Mating: Bats mate once a year.

Young: Newborn bats drink their mothers' milk. Some newborn bats hold on to their mothers.

Bats

Bats can fly, but they are not birds. All bats are mammals. Mammals are warm-blooded animals with a backbone. Warm-blooded means the animal's body heat stays the same. The body heat does not change with the outside weather.

Young bats are born alive. The newborns drink their mothers' milk.

There are more than 900 different kinds of bats. Each kind has its own features. Bats live almost everywhere. But bats cannot live in very hot or very cold weather.

All bats are nocturnal. This means they are active at night. This is when bats hunt for food. They sleep during the day.

Bats hang upside down while they sleep. Some bats sleep in caves or on tree branches. They have strong feet and sharp claws. These help them hold on to rock bumps or branches.

Bats hunt for food during the night.

Appearance

Bats are covered with fur. Their fur can be black, white, gray, yellow, brown, or red. Different kinds of bats are different features.

Some bats have large eyes. Other bats have tiny eyes. Bat ears are also different. Some are small and pointed. Others are long and large.

All bats have wings. Wings are made of two layers of skin. The skin is stretched between long, thin bones. Some bats' wings are pink and thin. These wings are thin enough to see through. Other bats have dark wings.

Some bats are small. The bumblebee bat in Thailand weighs less than a penny. Other bats are large. The gigantic flying fox is the largest bat in the world. It lives in Southeast Asia. Its wings can spread as wide as six feet (two meters).

All these features help bats live. Their eyes and ears help them find food in the dark.

Bats are covered with fur.

Where Bats Live

Bats live where other animals cannot find them. They live in bridges, attics, and caves. They live inside hollow tree trunks. Some bats hang from the branches of trees. The Honduran tent-making bat uses leaves to hide and sleep in.

Bats are warm-blooded animals. To live, their bodies must stay close to a certain temperature. Temperature is the amount of hot or cold in something. Bats pick roosts that are not too hot or too cold. A roost is a place where a bat can rest or sleep.

Bats hibernate in the winter. Hibernate means to spend the winter in a deep sleep. Bats choose a safe and warm place to hibernate. They usually hibernate in caves. Bats can die if a cave becomes too hot or too cold.

Hibernating bats wake up to stretch and clean themselves. They also get rid of waste from their bodies.

Some bats live in attics.

Sight and Sound

Bats wake up at night to hunt for food. They hunt when they are not hibernating. Many bats do not depend on their eyes to find food. Bats are not blind. Many bats have excellent vision. But bats use echolocation to help them hunt. Echolocation is using sound to locate objects and food.

Bats send out signals during echolocation. The signals are so high-pitched that humans cannot hear them. The signals bounce off objects and create echoes. An echo is the sound that returns after hitting an object. Echoes help bats know the size, speed, and direction of objects. Echolocation helps bats find food. It also helps bats avoid flying into things.

Echolocation is one of the reasons bats look the way they do. Bats have bumps on their faces, ears, and noses. The bumps help them hear the echoes. Echolocation works very well. Some bats can sense objects as thin as a human hair.

Bumps on their bodies help bats hear echoes.

Food

Bats' first food is their mothers' milk. Bats eat many different foods when they are older. In North America, many bats eat insects. A single little brown bat can eat 600 or more mosquitoes in one hour.

Some bats eat nectar. Nectar is a sweet liquid from flowers. Many bats eat fruit. The gigantic flying fox eats bananas, berries, and other fruits.

Still other bats eat fish, small lizards, and frogs. Fisherman bats live in South America. They use their their long, sharp claws to catch fish. Vampire bats drink blood from large animals. They sometimes drink blood from cows, horses, pigs, and large birds.

Sometimes a larger bat will eat a smaller bat. But this does not happen very often.

Some bats eat fruit.

Enemies

Bats have many enemies. Cats, weasels, snakes, and skunks eat bats. Owls, hawks, and other birds also eat bats.

Enemies wait at cave openings or other bat roosts. The enemies catch bats when they fly out at night. Bat hawks in Africa and the East Indies catch many bats. They catch the bats in their claws and swallow the bats whole.

Bats do not have many ways to keep safe. They must either fly away or hide.

People are also enemies of bats. Thousands of bats die each year from insecticides. An insecticide is a chemical used to kill insects. People spray insecticides on crops such as fruit. The insecticides keep insects from killing crops. Many of the bats eat the fruit, get sick, and die. Some people disturb bats in their roosts. They may catch or kill the roosting bats.

Sometimes people catch or kill roosting bats.

Young Bats

Most bats mate once each year. Females usually give birth in the spring or early summer.

Female bats raise the young. They often live in groups with other mothers and their young.

Some newborn bats hold on to their mothers. These newborn bats even hold on while their mothers fly and hunt.

Soon, the young bats become too heavy. The mothers then leave them behind at night. In the morning, the mothers return to their young.

Most bats can fly after about one month. Then they begin to hunt for their own food.

Young bats usually fly with their mothers for two weeks to a month. Then the young bats leave their mothers. Most female bats can have their own young at two years old.

Some newborn bats hold on to their mothers.